A PURBECK CHRISTMAS

A PURBECK CHRISTMAS

Compiled by
Rodney Legg

HALSGROVE

First published in 2002 by Halsgrove
Text © 2002 Rodney Legg

British Library Cataloguing-in-Publication Data
A CIP record for this title is available from the British Library

ISBN 1 84114 220 4

HALSGROVE

Halsgrove House
Lower Moor Way
Tiverton, Devon EX16 6SS
Tel: 01884 243242
Fax: 01884 243325
email: sales@halsgrove.com
website: www.halsgrove.com

Printed and bound in Great Britain by
Bookcraft (Bath) Ltd, Midsomer Norton

Contents

Preface

It's been rare for me to spend Christmas in Purbeck, mainly because of family commitments in Bournemouth, but since first cycling here – alone, as ever – at the age of eleven I've always made a pilgrimage to Corfe Castle and Tyneham over the short Army break that ends with New Year's Day. In relative maturity I've celebrated at pre-Christmas parties across the Isle of Purbeck, notably at the Manor Hotel, Studland, in sight of Fort Henry from which King George VI and future President of the United States Dwight D. Eisenhower watched live-fire rehearsals for the D-Day landings in 1944. That was on 18 April, the day that would happen to be my birthday, three years later.

As *Fawlty Towers* appeared on television I collected humorous anecdotes in country house hotels, though these never progressed beyond an essay on Holbrook House in Somerset, in which I was able to transfer some quotes from Studland. At the time the source would have been identifiable but anno domini has since removed any embarrassment. Christmas returnees at both Holbrook and Studland were from another England. For some there would always be a British Empire.

One delightful guest I met on the sands. She asked about the connection between the philosopher Bertrand Russell and Studland village and I pointed out Cliff End where he had seduced Lady Ottoline Morrell over the Easter holiday in 1911. Sex and politics were the ingredients because she was the wife of Liberal MP Philip Morrell. We compared contemporary scandals.

I'm afraid that at dinner I was still in jeans, navy-blue Guernsey and muddy trainers. They, of course, had dressed for the occasion and her uncle was a majestic Edwardian gentleman who looked the twin of Sir Edward Elgar. I have long ears for picking up the soft conversation of others across the room. After discussing the decay of civilisation and order in the Karen province of Burma their eyes glanced towards me.

'I think he lives with his cats,' she said, as if it explained everything. 'Do you like cats?' she asked him.

'Cats – we used to shoot them in the officers' mess in Ceylon. Must have shot a hundred of them. Vermin, when you get that many.'

In modern times my Purbeck days are usually spent in Swanage, where I have a parking space beside the Cluny Crescent home of Beata and George Willey, and find hospitality down in the High Street where their son Wolf and his wife Marie run the Red Lion. If I ask nicely she will show me her butterfly tattoo. In Station Road I'll call on Jill Blanchard and, around the corner, on Merle and Robert Chacksfield. I'm a bit like a country fox that comes into town for a comfort zone during the dark days of seasonal extremes.

One fox did just that when the 12-inch snowfall of Boxing Day in 1962 became freeze-dried by the most prolonged sub-zero temperatures of living memory. A glazed landscape glistened in the moonlight and the same snow lay on the ground for a record seventy days. During this time a hungry fox came down from the Townsend quarries and crossed urban Swanage to the seaside where it found itself on the pier. It could no longer go up, down, along or backwards. Sadly, this Christmas was to be its last.

My Purbeck, both here and in life, extends to the surrounding parishes of the district council area, to its public-house extremities of the Drax Arms in Bere Regis and the Frampton Arms at Moreton. I saw in the millennium at the former and return to the latter on Christmas Eve to greet Janette and John Paulson and fudge my vegetarianism by ordering scampi for Turbo the tortoiseshell cat.

This potted selection reflects my midwinter researches. There is hardly anything capable of being described as a happy Christmas in the work of Thomas Hardy. No wonder T.E. Lawrence missed out on the chance of spending it at Max Gate. Neither was it an auspicious one for starting the voyage that ended at Worth Matravers and provided source material for Charles Dickens. I have, however, spared you the almost annual record of deaths from exposure in the snow or even on top of the mail-coach. More cheerful things do find their place. There is nothing more redolent of the England of the last millennium than the Dorset carols that are sung at Bloxworth.

Accordian players: Christmas at the Frampton Arms, Moreton.

William Crowned on Christmas Day

Already hosting a Saxon royal house on the Castle Hill at Corfe Gate, Purbeck became a property of the Norman kings, providing marble for the building of cathedrals, a Royal Warren for rabbits and game, and the strategic site that evolved into one of the greatest fortresses in the land. All this stemmed from the victory of Duke William at 'La Place de Battell' near Hastings on 14 October 1066 and his subsequent progress to Berkhamstead, where the English submitted, the *Anglo-Saxon Chronicle* records:

Corfe Castle from a frosted gorse bush on East Hill, looking southwest over Corfe village and the valley mists to West Hill (right) and the hills between Steeple and Kimmeridge (left).

There he was met by Archbishop Aldred and Edgar Cild, and Earl Edwin and Earl Morcar, and all the chief men from London. And they submitted out of necessity after most damage had been done – and it was great piece of folly that they had not done it earlier, since God would not make things better, because of our sins. And they gave hostages and swore oaths to

Winter whites at Corfe Castle, northeastwards across Vineyard Farm from the hedgerow beside the Rings siege-work, which is also owned by the National Trust.

him, and he promised them he would be a gracious liege lord, and yet in the meantime they ravaged all that they overran. Then on Christmas Day, Archbishop Aldred consecrated him King at Westminster.

And he promised Aldred on Christ's book (before Aldred would place the crown on his head) that he would rule all this people as well as the best of kings before him, if they would be loyal to him. All the same he laid taxes on people very severely, and then went in spring overseas to Normandy, and took with him Archbishop Stigand, and Aethelnoth, Abbot of Glastonbury, and Edgar Cirl and Earl Edwin and Earl Morcar, and Earl Waltheof, and many other good men from England. And Bishop Odo and Earl William stayed behind and built castles far and wide throughout this country, and distressed the wretched folk, and always after that it grew much worse. May the end be good when God wills!

William the Conqueror had become King William I of England and would be succeeded through the millennium to his descendant who occupies the throne today – Queen Elizabeth II. Without knowing it at the time, Princess Elizabeth became Her Majesty the Queen while watching and filming Kenyan big game from Treetops Hotel, as her father died at Sandringham on the night of 5 February 1952. She celebrated her golden jubilee in 2002.

Corfe Castle from the scrubby slope of East Hill.

1678

The Phantom Army

In December 1678, Captain John Lawrence of Creech Grange, in the company of his brother and four clay-cutters, were astonished to see a hostile army of massive proportions marching along the top of the Purbeck Hills. They were coming from Flower's Barrow hill fort.

Captain Lawrence and his party fled to Wareham to raise the alarm and warning was sent to London, where Lawrence deposed the particulars on oath. He described a force of several thousand armed men, and in Wareham 300 militia were hastily marshalled to prepare to fight the invaders. The South Bridge was barricaded. Scouts were dispatched to reconnoitre the coast but they reported that they could find no sign of any army, nor the traces of any movements. The spectre of the Phantom Army, as it has come to be known, is believed to presage a national disaster.

Lawrence's loyalty to the Stuart crown must have been questioned and proved as beyond reproach. Otherwise he would have been spending Christmas in the Tower of London and looking forward to losing his head on Tower Hill.

Frosty evening beside the River Frome opposite Lady St Mary parish church at Wareham, looking westwards to the South Bridge (left).

New Christmas Day Proved Wrong

News has reached us from Christchurch that many people went into the New Forest to observe whether the oak, which is said to blow every Christmas Day, conforms to the new date for the festival on 25 December. Some pretended to be adamant that it would observe the new-style date but seemed in no way surprised to observe that no buds or any appearance of green leaves could be seen. Finding no such active buds they came away expressing dissatisfaction with the alteration of the day.

On their return the following Friday week, being the old-style date for Christmas, they were duly rewarded with the remarkable sight, and saw to their joy that the oak had blown. There were several branches and bows extending out into the clearing that were almost completely covered with green. This circumstance convinced them abundantly that the new Christmas Day is wrong and they vouched that henceforth they would keep only the genuine date of 5 January.

The Southern Times

Others later confirmed from Somerset that the same happened with the famous Glastonbury Thorn which had also 'blowed' as usual on the old-style day. Few attended markets that were held on Old Christmas Day.

Pope Gregory XIII had corrected the accumulation of small errors in the Roman calendar in 1582, by ordaining that 4 October was to be followed by 14 October, thereby acknowledging a solar year of 365 days 5 hours 49 minutes (rather than the 365 days 6 hours as fixed by Julius Caesar in 45BC and amended by Emperor Augustus with the device of a leap-year every four years to deal with the disparity in hours). Meanwhile, Britain carried on alone in classical time, with the result that defective minutes had accumulated into another erroneous day, by the time that London adopted the Gregorian calendar. The moment came at midnight on 2 September 1752, when dates were synchronised with those in Europe, with the result that not only was 3 September missing but the time became 00.00 hours on 14 September 1752. 'Give us back our eleven days,' was the cry of rioters in London but resentment lasted longest in the countryside, to the extent that fertility celebrations to wassail apple trees in the West Country still take place on Old Christmas Day.

Future miscalculations were avoided by juggling with centennial years, so that only those exactly divisible by 400 – such as 2000 – should be counted as leap years.

1762

Talk of a Christmas Star

The credulous were talking of a Christmas star in 1762 but the origin of the story has
been traced to Lulworth Castle at nine o'clock in the evening of the first Saturday in
December. There was a 'sudden and radiant light overspread the Earth and sea, equal to
the splendour of the noon-day Sun'. Witnesses said that looking 'directly perpendicular
over us we saw an appearance refulgent' – shining brightly – 'as the sun itself, in form
straight as a line'. It was about eight times the diameter of the moon in length, and had a
duration of a minute. 'Afterwards it altered its position, and changed into a serpentine
form, and seemed to terminate in smoke.'

1764

Swallows Don't Hibernate in Purbeck

Sir Peter Thompson of Poole wrote to the naturalist Peter Collinson (1694–1768) in 1764 to outline his documentation of the mass movement of swallows, with an account of his searches in nearby sandhills and the town's church tower. He also reports that the Purbeck quarrymen of Swanage and Langton Matravers assure him that they have never seen any of the swallow tribe either above or below ground in winter.

In his reply, Collinson told Sir Peter that neither do swallows hibernate by leaving 'the air to live under water (as Dr Linnaeus asserts) without some contrivance to their internal economy to qualify them for so great a chance of the elements'. Collinson's thoughts on the migration of swallows had been published in the *Philosophical Transactions* of 1760 but this shows that it was still an arguable matter in 1764.

1786

The Loss of the Halsewell

The *Halsewell* East-Indiaman, of 758 tons burden and commanded by Richard Pierce, was ordered by the directors of the East-India Company to prepare for her third voyage to Bengal, at their meeting on 16 November 1785. She was brought down the Thames to Gravesend to complete loading over Christmas. On Christmas Eve, Lieutenant James Brymer RN married the daughter of his senior officer, Captain Norman, and joined the voyage to visit his uncle in Madras. As their father, Rev. Francis Humphries, took seasonal services at Hampstead, brothers James and William persuaded Captain Pierce to take them on as midshipmen, on the recommendation of a mutual friend, and had only hours to prepare for the voyage of a lifetime. By the end of the festivities the passengers, including ladies, were taken on board at the Hope.

Richard Pierce was the oldest of the East-India Company's pilots and he planned to retire on his return. The passengers included his daughters, Eliza Pierce and Mary Anne Pierce, with their cousins from Somerset, Amy Paul and Mary Paul. They were also related to Thomas Burston, the chief mate. Miss Elizabeth Blackborne was the daughter of another East-India captain. Miss Mary Haggard was the sister of an officer in the Madras establishment. Miss Anne Mansel was born in Madras, of European parents, and was returning on completion of schooling in England. John George Schutz was returning to Asia to collect his residual fortune.

The unfolding story is told by two of her officers, second mate Henry Meriton and third mate John Rogers, who described what promised to be a happy and prosperous voyage. *Halsewell* was one of the finest ships in the service and in tip-top condition. Her captain was an exemplary character of distinguished ability.

They proceeded to sail through the Downs on New Year's Day, Sunday 1 January 1786. The next morning, abreast of Dunnose, it fell calm. At 15.00 hours a breeze sprang up from the south and they ran inshore to try and land the pilot. Thick weather, however, came on in the evening. At 21.00 hours they were obliged to anchor in 18 fathoms of water and furled the top-sails, but could not do the same with the courses as snow was falling fast and freezing as it fell.

On Tuesday 3 January, at 04.00 hours, a strong gale developed from east-north-east and the ship began to drive. They were obliged to cut their cables and run off to sea. At noon the *Halsewell* drew alongside a brig heading for Dublin and transferred the pilot to her. Then they bore down the Channel. Darkness brought a freshening wind from the south and at 20.00 hours they reefed such sails as were judged necessary. By 22.00 hours this had turned into a violent gale and a press of sail was needed to keep the ship offshore. The hawse plugs, which had only recently been reset inside the vessel, were washed in. As the hawse bags were washed away a large quantity of water was shipped across the gun-deck.

On sounding the well, they found the ship had sprung a leak, with 5 feet of water in the hold. All the pumps were set to work. They then 'clued' the main top-sail up, hauled up the main-sail, and attempted to furl both. Neither would open.

The emergency became a crisis at 02.00 hours on Wednesday, 4 January. They endeavoured to wear the ship, without success, and remove the mizzen mast. A second attempt to wear the ship was also unsuccessful. Soundings of the well showed that they were taking water faster than the pumps could empty it. There was now 7 feet of water in the hold and they were in immediate danger of foundering.

The next desperate measure to try and preserve the ship was the order to cut away the main mast. In doing so, coxswain, Jonathan Moreton, and four men were either drawn or fell overboard, and drowned. At 08.00 hours, in first light, the wreck of the mast was cleared and the ship seemed to have been saved, as she got before the wind and maintained this state for two hours, during which the pumps made progress with the water in the hold problem, reducing its level to 5 feet. Using just the fore-sail the head of the ship was brought to point eastwards.

At 10.00 hours the wind abated considerably and the ship laboured extremely. The fore top-mast rolled over on the larboard [starboard] side and smashed through the fore-sail. The wind then backed to the westward at 11.00 hours as the weather cleared. Berry Head was identified, to the northeast, four or five leagues distant. They now bent another fore-sail and erected a jury main-mast, setting a top-gallant-sail for a main-sail. With these they bore for Portsmouth and used the remainder of the day in getting up a jury mizzen-mast.

Thursday, 5 January, at 02.00 hours, the wind came to the south and blew fresh with the weather thickening. Portland was seen to the northeast at noon and was distant 2 or 3 leagues. At night, at 20.00 hours, it blew a strong gale from the south and the Portland lights were seen bearing northwest at 4 or 5 leagues. They got the ship heading westward but found they were losing ground on that tack and wore her again. She kept stretching on eastward and they hoped to have passed Peveril Point, at Swanage, in which case they intended anchoring in Studland Bay.

At 23.00 hours the sky cleared and they saw they were still further west, with St Alban's Head a mile and a half leeward, and they took in sail immediately. They also let go the small bower anchor which brought up the ship at a whole cable, but then drove. They let go the sheet anchor and wore away a whole cable. The ship rode for about two hours longer and then she drove again.

Captain Richard Pierce sent for Henry Meriton and asked his opinion on the chances of saving their lives. Calmly and with candour he replied that there was little hope. 'We are driving fast on shore,' he said, 'and may expect every moment to strike.' It was agreed that the boats were of no use at that time, but in case an opportunity arose, the long-boat should be reserved for the ladies and the officers. This was to be kept confidential.

Pierce and Meriton spoke again in the cuddy at 02.00 hours on Friday, 6 January. The ship was still driving and they were approaching alarmingly fast to the shore. Captain Pierce expressed extreme anxiety for the preservation of his beloved daughters. Meriton said the only hope was that they might wait for morning, on which the captain was silent and lifted his hands in a gesture of distress.

At that moment the ship struck with such violence as to dash the heads of those who were standing in the cuddy, against the deck above them, and the fatal blow was accompanied by a shriek of horror, which burst at that instant from every quarter of the ship. Many of the seamen were in their bunks, having left most of the exertions of pumping to the officers and the soldiers, and now streamed on to the deck. Some climbed the ensign staff thinking the ship would break up immediately. She continued to beat on the rocks. Her hull bulged and she fell broadside towards the shore.

Halsewell *tragedy: the end of the outward-bound East Indiaman on the cliffs at Seacombe, a few days into the New Year in 1786.*

In this crisis of horror, Meriton urged the crew to descend to the side of the ship lowest to the rocks, and attempt their escape. Meanwhile the ladies and most of the officers had gathered in the round-house and attempted to gain comfort in the thought that they might all be saved if the ship held together till the morning. They knew the ship was between St Alban's Head and Peveril Point on the island of Purbeck where high cliffs rose almost perpendicular. Its precise location was on the west side of Seacombe.

Here the cliff is excavated at its foot, by the waves, with a cavern of 10 or 12 yards in depth, and of breadth equal to the length of a large ship. Its sides are nearly upright and the roof formed by a stupendous clifftop, making the cavern difficult

Seacombe Cliffs: the rock-face that confronted the Halsewell victims and survivors, at night in a January gale.

of access, with the bottom strewn with sharp and uneven rocks. The wreck lay stretched across the length of this horrid chasm.

It was too dark to discover these details. The seamen demanded entrance to the round-house, to get the lights, but were kept out by Mr Rogers, the third mate, and Mr Brymer, the fifth mate. The company did admit three black women and two soldiers' wives. There were near 50 in number gathered around Captain Pierce, with a daughter on each side of him. He alternately pressed each to his affectionate bosom. The rest of the melancholy assembly were seated on the deck. It was strewn with musical instruments, broken furniture, trunks, boxes and packages.

Mr Meriton cut wax candles into pieces and stuck them around the round-house. All the glass lanterns were also lit. A basket of oranges was passed around and the ladies were prevailed on to refresh themselves by sucking a little juice. They were tolerably composed, except Miss Mansel, who was in hysterical fits on the floor.

On leaving the round-house in the stern, Meriton found the ship was in an increasingly distressed state. Its sides were breaking, the deck lifting, and the hull separating in the middle. Realising that the fore part of the ship was moving seawards, Mr Meriton decided that his best hope was to join the crew and soldiers, who had made their way to the shore. Burmaster, a seaman, passed him a lanthorn through the sky-light of the round-house. He discovered a spar between the ship's side and the rocks.

Crawling along it, Meriton found it actually made no contact with the land, as he slipped off the end. He was badly bruised and caught in a surging wave, swimming with it into the cavern, where he failed to gain a hold until a hand stretched out to him from the back wall and dragged him from the sea.

Mr Rogers had remained with the captain and the ladies in the round-house. Miss Mary Pierce, in particular, was apprehensive that Mr Meriton had been lost. 'Oh poor Meriton,' another lady said. 'He is drowned. Had he stayed with us he would have been safe.'

They were reluctant to allow Rogers to go out in search of him. Instead he received a nod from Captain Pierce and the pair took up a lamp and inspected the stern gallery. They could see no way of escape and Pierce, with his greatcoat on, returned to sit down between his daughters as the sea continued to break in fast. Mr Rogers was approached by McManus, a midshipman, and Mr Schutz, a passenger, and asked what they could do. 'Follow me,' Rogers said, as he led them to the stern gallery and by the weather upper quarter-gallery upon the poop, at the moment when a heavy sea fell on board and caused the round-house to collapse. They heard the ladies shriek at intervals as if the sea had reached them.

Mr Brymer had followed Mr Rogers to the poop. The same wave that was fatal to those below had lifted a hen-coop which they seized as it carried them to a large rock. Though badly bruised they found they were among 27 taking refuge there. Fearing being washed off by a rising tide, they left it for the back or sides of cavern. Scarce more than six, including Brymer and Rogers, managed to reach comparative safety on the narrow shelves. There they found a considerable number of the crew, seamen, soldiers and some petty officers.

They had escaped immediate death but were to experience cold, nakedness, wind, rain and the perpetual beating of spray. All visible traces of the wrecked ship had gone. Before they struck the rocks, they had fired their guns in distress to alarm the country, but the violence of the storm meant that they were unheard. Neither could they be seen from above as they languished in the cavern. No ropes could reach them there or boat approach to search them out. The only escape was to creep to the outward extremity of the cavern and move along a ledge scarcely as broad as a man's hand. Then they would have to turn the corner and clamber up the perpendicular precipice. Some succeeded in this endeavour but others lost their precarious footing and perished in the attempt.

The ship's cook and John Thompson, a quarter-master, were the first to the top. They made their way up the valley to the nearest house, Eastington Farm, which was the home of Mr Goddard, a steward to the proprietors of the Purbeck Quarries. He called together his workmen and gathered quarry ropes, with the most zealous and animated humanity, and exerted every effort in the preservation of the surviving crew. Mr Meriton had a close call. The stone that was his foothold gave way at the very moment he grabbed a rope and was safely drawn to the summit.

Mr Brymer was less fortunate. Numbed and trembling with the cold, he failed to fasten the rope properly, and fell and was dashed to pieces during the rescue attempt. His loss was a particular tragedy, as he had married only a week before they sailed, on Christmas Eve. It saddened everyone but there would have been many more casualties but for the skill of the Purbeck quarrymen. They coped with the 100-foot precipice and an 8-foot projection at the top by stationing another two daring fellows – ropes tied around them, fastened to a strong iron bar fitted in the ground – who leant into the wind from the outcrop and let down another rope with a noose which the would-be survivor had to put around his waist. Then he was pulled into a full swing, dangling, being drawn up beside the jagged rocks with great care and caution.

One of the saddest losses was a young drummer who was washed seawards and kept swimming but was carried by counter-seas or reverse waves until he finally succumbed to exhaustion beyond the breakers. Thomas Jeane, a midshipman, was also in and out of the waves for seven hours before he perished. All day the quarrymen continued their efforts and returned the following day for the last soldier, William Trenton, who maintained his perilous stand until Saturday, 7 January.

There was no sign of any section of ship but fragments and debris were everywhere including the remains of a single sheep from the livestock of the unfortunate officers. The muster of men in Mr Garland's house now reached 74, out of a total of 242 who had set sail; the death-toll was 168. Two or three of them had died while being lifted, and a coloured man had died at Eastington, where many were nursing horrific bruises. All the ship's documentation was lost.

Meriton and Rogers set off for London on the Saturday and arrived with the grim news at India House at noon on Sunday, 8 January. The directors ordered handsome gratifications to the Purbeck quarrymen. They received 100 guineas to be distributed among them. Such heroism mitigated national feelings of disaster as families grieved across the land. The losses included the two young men from Hampstead who had decided on impulse over Christmas to sail to find their fame and fortune. Folklore and wreck-diving have kept the memory of the *Halsewell* alive.

Cold Christmas
to Christmas Peacock

The *Journal of Mary Frampton*, of Moreton House, records that the cold came at Christmas and the months of January and February remained very severe and 'much suffering attended the state of the poor from the preceding summer having been too wet to enable them to get in their turf for fuel'. Rights of turbary were still being exercised across the heaths – indeed there is a Turbary Common at Wallisdown, Bournemouth – with peat-spades being used to extract blocks of semi-decomposed vegetation from the moors. In remoter heathland parts, such as beside the little schoolroom provided by Lady Calcraft for the hamlet of Bushey near Rempstone, there used to be a stack of such fuel beside the building into living memory. 'Villages in these districts, where turf constitutes the common fuel, were particularly ill off,' Mary Frampton writes.

She goes on to record that the cold continued until 23 March 1830. Then, until All Fools Day at the start of April, the temperature soared and 'the weather was most extraordinarily warm and bright'. The thermometer at noon reached between 63°F and 67°F. Then, on 1 April, 'a considerable fall of snow began, which continued for many hours, lying some inches deep on the ground'.

From Windsor and London 'much murmuring' concerned the health of the monarch, King George IV, with expectations that he would be well enough 'to have a Drawing-room on St George's Day'. However, as 23 April approached, the first bulletin was issued. The secrecy as to what was happening at Windsor Castle remained 'quite impenetrable, and left a wide field for numerous conjectures of all kinds'. Sir William Knighton handled the situation and postponed the scheduled final consecration of two bishops at the end of the

Moreton House: the home of the Frampton family, with a stork as a winter visitor.

month. Parliament passed a bill to enable measures to be stamped on the King's behalf as 'the arrears of signatures' were 'said to amount to some thousands'.

Springtime was turning into a continuation of a long winter. There was no prospect of the nation's social life resuming with 'everybody in London afraid of naming distant days for their balls and parties, lest the expected death of the King should put a stop to all gaiety'. Instead they flocked to the opera, where Madame Lalande 'was the new woman' and Mademoiselle Taglioni the top dancer, late in the season. The King would linger until 26 June.

His notable legacy to the Royal Family was the conversion of Buckingham House into Buckingham Palace though with lasting concern that 'the entrance and basement storeys' were 'much too low'. George IV had insisted upon this, 'liking to inhabit low rooms himself; and this has injured the effect of the whole building'. Its saving grace was regarded as Marble Arch, between Birdcage Walk and the entrance, until this was removed to its present location, at Hyde Park Corner, in 1851.

The year of 1830 would turn into that of the agricultural riots, with labourers demanding higher wages and torching machinery, and Mary's brother, landowner James Frampton, led 'the Constabulary force' in their suppression. After incidents at Bere Regis and Lulworth, and the reading of the Riot Act near Winfrith Newburgh, threats were made against Frampton's home.

Moreton House remained in a state of siege until Christmas which was celebrated with 'a large family party'. Charles Wollaston, having visited his step-brother, James Frampton, found the building 'barricaded like an Irish mansion'. Mary Frampton rounds off the story:

> The house was unbarred and unblockaded with the exception of one large window on the staircase. The carol singers from Mr Frampton's own parishes ushered in Christmas Eve and Christmas Morn as usual, but no mummers were allowed to perform their ancient dramas of the wonderful recovery of a man killed in battle by a little elixir drawn from the pocket of the doctor of the piece, or to personify the 'Senses' from the ancient mysteries with their Latin names, 'Tactus', 'Visus' etc. The Yule log, however, burnt on the large hearth of the entrance hall. The peacock, in full plumage with its fiery mouth, was placed on the dinner table with, of course, the boar's head; the immense candles were well covered with laurel. The hare appeared with the red herring astride on its back, and the wassail bowl and lamb's wool were not inferior to former years.

1846

Carols and Perils at Swanage

John Mowlem (1788–1868), the Swanage-born contractor who paved London streets and founded Mowlem plc, records that 'lots of people were begging' in his home town on Christmas Eve in 1846. It was a Thursday, according to the diary edited by David Lewer:

We have given away lots of beef and pence to the poor. The night was cold, the singers as usual sang their Christmas carol, one of Mr Joseph Manwell's. He, poor man, had the idea he could compose music and passed a great deal of time in arranging its score. His sons were his band. He sang as well as he could, then found fault, then sang again, then altered a few notes until some of the quick passages looked as black as a thundercloud. He did his best and all his arts were moral but he was not a master of music.

So to Friday, and Christmas Day, with a quarter moon. Mowlem notes that a strong and cold northeasterly wind blew straight into Swanage Bay during the morning. A Revenue cutter is on the North Ledge with her head facing northwest. High-water came at 14.00 hours and the vessel is identified as the *Petrel* from Weymouth. Her plight is causing concern:

She strikes heavily and if the wind should increase there will be loss of life. The men ought to be allowed to leave her for, as she is in broken water, how are boats to get alongside in a gale of wind? John Soper, of the *Gertrude*, with his boat's crew, today would have been swamped if they had not been expert. Three or four heavy seas rose nearly at the same time and broke very heavily near them; but all was well managed.

The approach to the old pier at Swanage in January 1895, before construction started on the present pier, with the Olive Branch *stone-boat beached and wrecked by heavy icing in the background.*

Mowlem dined with his wife, Susannah Manwell, and Miss Fowler and Miss Browse, enjoying their usual 'roast beef of old England and plum pudding'. John was then left to spend the evening alone, 'all hands' having gone to the home of Susannah's sister, Mrs Laetitia Burt, at No.1 Victoria Terrace, 'and the maids to see their friends'. Laetitia was the wife of Robert Burt and their son, George, was making his fortune in London.

The un-festive story for the *Petrel* ends well. She is released from the rocks on Saturday, Boxing Day, and taken in tow by Soper and the *Gertrude* cutter to her base at Custom House Quay in Weymouth: 'So far all is well, but there was great danger of swamping the boats in broken water.'

Mowlem returns to the plight of the poor on 29 December:

I have made out a list from Swanage poor to receive rice at two-pence per pound and salt-fish at one penny per pound. There will be a loss on this but we pay this loss by subscription from the inhabitants. I wrote Mr Stamp asking for money out of my own pocket which is too bad of him to allow me to ask.

Swanage Bay at dawn on the calmest of winter days, looking northeast to Ballard Point from a groyne near New Swanage.

1851

The Swanage Riot

The first Swanage policeman, John Cripps, was 'nearly killed' on Monday, 24 December 1851. John Mowlem records the 'Christmas Eve riot' and its aftermath:

There was a mob of boys and men to the number of 100, and had it not been for Mrs Melmoth I think the poor fellow must have lost his life. I was half a day yesterday [Friday, 26 December] at the Rectory with Dr Wilcox and Mr Serrell taking the depositions of sundry persons respecting the attack. I sincerely hope the guilty will be brought to justice and transported if possible. William Croft is the ring-leader of the party and a worse man there cannot be. He is a bad husband and a drunkard to boot. There are issued three summons to appear next Tuesday before the magistrates at Wareham.

He goes on to note that 'idle people about the street are rather more dull today' and ponders that 'they fancy there is a rod in pickle for them'. Mowlem laments that 'unless something can be done to protect the quiet inhabitants of this place, all that can move away from it will do so. I often regret I settled down here.'

This was certainly his opinion on Tuesday, 30 December:

The rioters of this place were taken before the bench of magistrates at Wareham and fined £2 10s 0d. Five were taken to Dorchester Prison but on payment of the fine will be released. William Croft was fined £5 0s 0d. He ought to have been sent to the sessions. The magistrates don't know their duty. I look at them as a set of old ladies. A fine for the rabble here is of no use. The inhabitants are 500 years behind the times and those who sit in judgement are further still.

The following day, New Year's Eve, John Mowlem bestowed his customary charity on the respectable old men of the town. A total of 22 gathered for a good dinner:

All that were there this day twelve-month were alive to this day. I close the year with gratitude to God for all his mercies.

1867

Oxen Kneeling in the Stalls

In these insular parts it is still believed among country people that at midnight on Christmas Eve the oxen in their stalls go on their knees in attitudes of devotion. Many a farmer in the Isle of Purbeck will declare that he has watched them, and has seen some, at least, of his oxen fall upon their knees at or about that hour, and make a 'moan like Christian Creatures'. There is an old print of the nativity in which the oxen in the stable, near the Virgin and the Child, are represented on their knees in a suppliant posture. It is well known that an ox and an ass are recorded to have been in the stable at the time of the birth of Jesus Christ.

Another notion is that cocks, at the season of Christmas, crow all night long, to free the country of evil spirits against the Feast of the Nativity. During the season of midwinter cocks are often particularly vociferous, especially in the dark, still, open weather. Shakespeare refers to this superstition in the opening scene of Hamlet:

> Some say that even 'gainst the hallowed season,
> At which our Saviour's birth is celebrated,
> The birds of dawning croweth all night long.

Weymouth, Portland and Dorchester Telegram

1868

Coal Concern at the Christmas Fireside

Christmas Day, this Friday, was fine and bright, which brought relief after a month prolific of heavy gales. That of one Sunday night, 7 December 1868, was a tornado, which began shortly after midnight and maintained its fury for three hours. For most of us, the festivities have been put off to Boxing Day, which was fine in the morning but has turned wet and boisterous this afternoon.

The cost of coal is a major topic of Christmas conversation in Poole and thereabouts where they envy the ease in which this vital commodity is shipped into Swanage with the very best Walls End Coal being available at 19s 0d a ton. There the stone trade brings boats from London and their profitable incoming ballast is coal from Newcastle. Poole has no such convenient arrangement and Bournemouth, we hear, fares even worse. Inland coals can scarcely be brought to Bournemouth without a railway. Occasionally, but recently rarely, a barge is drawn up on the beach, but otherwise they rely on supplies brought by cart from Poole.

This is of concern to everyone in remoter parts of Purbeck and the Southern Coast when the sun goes down blurred and early. Home travellers are bitterly cold, and shudder in the wintry blast, as they gaze wearily on the gloomy evening landscape. People on the quays and in the streets bend down their heads and run before the weather. Wandering snow flakes sting us as they alight on our eyelids. In rustic places mists arise from fen and dyke and river. The high wet fern, the sodden moss, the beds of damp fallen leaves, all contribute to discomfort. Trees are lost to view in masses of impenetrable shade. As the long night sets all is dark and dreary.

Our great consolation is the fireside. When the mill has stopped, when the village black-smith shuts his workshop, when the plough and harrow are left lonely in the fields, the labourer goes home to enjoy his fire. Lights from the cottage windows are the only cheer-ful sights in the countryside. Gas lamps in the streets and shops are the greatest consola-tion in our towns; except, indeed, the glowing fires in the kitchens, at which the Christmas sirloin or New Year's turkey may be roasting, exhaling fragrances which sharpen up the appetites and set passing pedestrians exclaiming loudly for their dinners.

Poole and Purbeck should be supplied with moderately-priced sea-borne coal. It can be procured from Shields, Sunderland, Hartlepool, Cardiff or Liverpool at easy rates. Our own shipping should bring us this easy supply. The reason that they are not doing so may lie in the fact that coal is now so cheap at the collieries, arising from the excessively hot summer we have just enjoyed, and the consequent accumulation of fuel at the pit's mouth. 'Coals, Coals, Coals!' say dealers' advertisements without ever mentioning their price. Yet it is 'price' that is at the basis of this question.

Shippers say that it is no longer economic for them to move coal in competition to the railway and point out that Poole is now linked by the Somerset and Dorset line to the Somersetshire Coalfield between Radstock and Bath. But it is remarkable how little that railway does, comparatively, to distribute the supply of coal or to meet our demand for it. We ought to have Somersetshire Coal at a price not exceeding 12s 0d a ton. Not only should we profit by the increased supply, but the competition between a large and effec-tive supply of inland and sea-borne coals would clearly result in a diminution of the price of the latter. The Somersetshire description of coal does not yet enjoy public favour in our neighbourhood. The rich and well-to-do use it once and return to a higher-priced article from much further afield, to which they have all their lives been accustomed. They prefer, they say, the comparative freedom of dust from their 'Derby Brights' to an economised shilling or two in price per ton.

The poorer classes, stinting their fires with any kind of coals they may obtain, get less brightness and light from the Somersetshire than the Northern products. It will be a long time, yet, before mere cheapness in price convinces the patrons of dwarf-fires that they have the privilege of putting cheapness and increased comfort in one scale. Custom and habit are as ineradicable in this respect as any other.

The *Southern Times*

1875

Thomas Hardy 'Once at Swanage'

Dorset's already acclaimed thirty-five-year-old author was lodging in Swanage at the West End Cottage home of Captain Joseph Masters where he completed *The Hand of Ethelberta* over Christmas in 1875. *Far from the Madding Crowd* had gone through highly popular magazine serialisation and sold out its first two-volume edition in a couple of months at the start of the year. It was their first real home together for newly married Thomas Hardy and Emma Gifford. They had married in St Peter's Church, Paddington, on 17 September 1874, spent the night at the Palace Hotel, Queensway, and honeymooned in Brighton en route for Dieppe, Rouen and Paris. Three nights in Bournemouth in July 1875 were followed by a paddle-steamer journey to Swanage followed by ten months by the Purbeck seaside before they found a longer-term home overlooking the River Stour at Sturminster Newton.

In Swanage, Hardy was thinking himself into his character Ethelberta Chickerel, who was a female mirror image of himself. It displays Hardy and England's great obsession with class. Ethelberta was a writer and poet from a servant family who hides her humble origins as she indulges the high life and glides through intellectual society, disguising herself as the enigmatic widow Ethelberta Petherwin. Hardy empathised so well with women that it was seriously suggested that his books were actually written by a woman and that 'she' was doing another George Eliot. We would have known so much more of Hardy in Purbeck but for his own bonfires of history and the later massaging of the record by second wife Florence.

One entry from Hardy's otherwise destroyed diaries has survived, recycled into his biography, and includes a phrase incorporated in his poem celebrating first wife Emma and Thomas's time in Swanage:

Moody moment: Hardy, the poet, and Florence Dugdale, his second wife, contemplate the sea.

Evening just after sunset. Sitting with Emma on a stone under the wall before the Refreshment Cottage. On the left Durlston Head roaring high and low, like a giant asleep. On the right a thrush. Above the bird hangs a new Moon, and a steady planet.

The roar of Durlston, which still had an active blow-hole until disturbance by late-nineteenth-century quarrying and construction work, features in 'Once at Swanage':

> The spray sprang up across the cusps of the Moon,
> And all its light loomed green
> As a witch-flame's weirdsome sheen
> At the minute of an incantation scene;
> And it greened our gaze – that night at demilune.
>
> Roaring high and roaring low was the sea
> Behind the headland shores;
> It symboled the slamming of doors,
> Or a regiment hurrying over hollow floors…
> And there two stood, hands clasped, I and she!

Another poetic record of Durlston Head is contained in 'To a Sea-Cliff' where Emma and Thomas are also pictured within, as 'a silent listless pair' in a precursor to the moods and paranoia to come:

> Lend me an ear
> While I read you here
> A page from your history,
> Old cliff – not known
> To your solid stone,
> Yet yours inseparably.

Near to your crown
There once sat down
A silent listless pair;
And the sunset ended,
And dark descended,
and still the twain sat there.

Past your jutting head
Then a line-ship sped,
Lit brightly as a city;
And she sobbed: 'There goes
a man who knows
I am his, beyond God's pity!'

He did apart
Who had thought her heart
His own, and not aboard
A barque, sea-bound…
That night they found
Between them lay a sword.

Swanage Cliffs is also given as the location for 'The Sunshade':

Ah – it's the skeleton of a lady's sunshade,
Here at my feet in the hard rock's chink,
Merely a naked sheaf of wires! –
Twenty years have gone with their livers and diers
Since it was silked in its white or pink.

Noonshine riddles the ribs of the sunshade,
No more a screen from the weakest ray;

Nothing to tell us the hue of its dyes,
Nothing but rusty bones as it lies
In its coffin of stone, unseen till to-day.

Where is the woman who carried that sunshade
Up and down this seaside place? –
Little thumb standing against its stem,
Thoughts perhaps bent on a love stratagem,
Softening yet more the already soft face!

Is the fair woman who carried that sunshade
A skeleton just as her property is,
Laid in the chink that none may scan?
And does she regret – if regret dust can –
The vain things thought when she flourished this?

1899

'A Christmas Ghost Story', by Thomas Hardy

South of the Line, inland from Durban,
A mouldering soldier lies – your countryman.
Awry and doubled up are his gray bones,
And on the breeze his puzzled phantom moans
Nightly to clear Canopus: 'I would know
By whom and when All-Earth-gladdening Law
Of Peace, brought by that Man Crucified,
Was ruled to be inept, and set aside?
And what of logic or truth appears
In tacking "Anno Domini" to the years
Near twenty-hundred liveried thus have hied,
But tarries yet the Cause for which He died.'

1900
Christmas Customs Old and New

The Christmas Bull at Shillingstone was a man dressed in a bull's head who would be navigated around the village by his 'Keeper' and visit Christmas parties. A less attractive Christmas practice, put into action in the New Forest on Boxing Day was 'squocking' or 'skuggy hunting' for red squirrels which were noisily chased from one block of woodland to the next. As they attempted to jump across the rides they were brought down by sticks and stones and killed by dogs as they fell to the ground. Before the Great War squirrel feasts were held at Burley, with much drinking, as the bodies were consumed by fire. It shows just how far the world has changed, now that the last of these animals are cherished as an endangered species on Brownsea Island, and that not all change has been for the worse.

1909

'The House of Hospitalities', by Thomas Hardy

Here we broached the Christmas barrel,
Pushed up the charred log-ends;
Here we sang the Christmas carol,
And called in friends.

Time has tired me since we met here
When the folk now dead were young,
Since the viands were outset here
And quaint songs sung.

And the worm has bored the viol
That used to lead the tune,
Rust eaten out the dial
That struck night's noon.

Now no Christmas brings in neighbours,
And the New Year comes unlit;
Where we sang the mole now labours,
And spiders knit.

Yet at midnight if here walking,
When the moon sheets wall and tree,
I see the form of old time talking
Who smile on me.

'The Prospect',
by Thomas Hardy

The twigs of the birch imprint the December sky
Like branching veins upon a thin old hand;
I think of summer-time, yes, of last July,
When she was beneath them, greeting a gathered band
Of the urban and bland.

Iced airs wheeze through the skeletoned hedge from the north,
With steady snores, and a numbing that threatens snow,
And skaters pass; and merry boys go forth
To look for slides. But well, well do I know
Whither I would go!

1914

Rupert Brooke at Blandford and Lulworth

Soldier-poet Rupert Brooke who adopted Lulworth and wrote his famous lines at Blandford Camp in 1914.

Dorset figures as much as Cambridge in the landscape and life of the soldier-poet Rupert Brooke (1887–1915) whose last Christmas was spent at Blandford Camp. As Sub-Lieutenant Rupert Brooke of the Hood Battalion of the Royal Naval Division, in the huts of the Anson Line, he had arrived in mid-December. 'Send mince-pies for 60 men and a few cakes immediately,' he telegrams to a friend. This was followed by a letter describing the first Christmas of the Great War:

I spend Christmas in looking after drunken stokers. One of them has been drunk since seven am; he neither eats nor drinks, but dances a complicated step up and down in his hut, singing, 'How happy I am, how happy I am' – a short, fat inelegant man, in stockinged feet. What wonders we are! There's no news – occasional scares. On Wednesday I (don't tell a soul) started a sonnet. What a fall!

The five sonnets were entitled '1914'. Their author was moving in high political circles, staying with Lady Wimborne at Canford House and at No. 10 Downing Street on a visit to London. He knew Winston Churchill through his Asquith and Guest family connections. Churchill visited Blandford Camp, as First Lord of the Admiralty, on 18 February 1915 and took the salute on a march-past in the rain. King George V followed in secret on 25 February to wish them well as they embarked on the misadventure to capture the Dardanelles from the Turks.

He sailed from Avonmouth on the *Grantully Castle* on 28 February. In the event, after going the length of the Mediterranean to Cairo, it was en route to the Gallipoli peninsula that a different fate intervened. It was through blood poisoning from an insect bite, among the flowering sage and big tortoises of the idyllic island of Skyros, rather than in the fiercely contested landings, that the prophetic words of 'The Soldier' came to pass.

Rupert Brooke died and was buried on Friday 23 April – the day of St George and Shakespeare – in the olive-grove where he had sat on the Tuesday of that week, between the mountains of Paphko, Komaro and Khokilas:

If I should die, think only this of me:
  That there's some corner of a foreign field
That is for ever England…

The 'poet-soldier' became idolised, with Winston Churchill calling him one of 'England's noblest sons' in his obituary for *The Times* on 26 April 1915. Yeats had described him as 'the handsomest man in England'. D.H. Lawrence parodied him 'as a Greek god under a Japanese sunshade, reading poetry in his pyjamas'.

He was 'a professional charmer' according to Leonard Woolf, husband of Virginia, who as the 'Wolves' or 'Wolf Pack' adopted Studland for their alternative Bloomsbury-by-Sea. Rupert Brooke had adopted Lulworth, where John Keats had written a sonnet. So had Rupert, on 8 July 1907, entitled Pine-trees and the sky – evening, after writing: 'Tomorrow

I'm going to the most beautiful place in England to work. It is called West Lulworth.' It was 'a favourite resort of the cycling confraternity' and, he told his mother, 'I do a fair amount of work here.' He did less, however, than at Bournemouth where he also stayed, and he found comparisons irresistible: 'No promenades, nor lifts, nor piers, nor a band.'

Rooms for Rupert and his friends were arranged through Lulworth's postmaster, Henry Joseph Chaffey, who also owned apartments. Pals from Cambridge and Rugby enjoyed an 'hilarious' vacation with 'reading parties'. He wrote to his mother:

> One day we were reading on the rocks, and I had a Keats in my pocket, but it slipped out, and, falling into a swift current, was borne out to sea. So we leapt into a boat and rowed up and down the coast till we espied it off some rocks. But the sea was rather rough and we could not land on the rocky part, or get near Keats. So we landed half a mile off the beach, and came over the rocks to the Keats, and when we found it, I stripped and went in after it and got it. It is indeed quite spoilt; but it only cost two shillings to begin with.

It was not until years later, in 1911, that Rupert Brooke heard of the connection between Keats and Lulworth Cove. The poet was becalmed and made his last landfall in England, in September 1820, while coughing blood and sailing towards death in Rome. Rupert found this coincidence 'the most amazing thing'.

A different Rupert Brooke at Lulworth emerges from his biography by Nigel Jones in 1999. He is less charismatic and more ordinary, though still talented, and both devious and randy. In Lulworth, apparently, he was going through a mental breakdown which affected him profoundly. He suffered from insomnia and acted like 'a spoilt, self-pitying brat'.

His friend Geoffrey Keynes deleted references to himself from Rupert's letters. Henry Lamb was at Lulworth with him and callously scorned Rupert's efforts at seduction. Rupert's suppressed correspondence, kept under wraps by the British Library until 2000, abounds in four-letter words. Later, it is claimed, he fathered an illegitimate child by a Tahitian woman who writes to him: 'I get fat, all the time, sweetheart.'

Another of a succession of overlapping affairs was with Phyllis Gardner. The pair swam together naked at Grantchester and then made love in a field. All this adds passion and interest to a life that used to seem a little too good to be true. His fateful return to Dorset in the Great War, with midwinter visits to Tarrant Crawford Abbey and Badbury Rings, also revived memories of holidays in Bournemouth, with his grandfather, Rev. Richard England Brooke.

Coincidentally, his home was called Grantchester Dene, and Rupert would live at Grantchester, Cambridge, where he wrote 'The Old Vicarage' about the house which is now the home of Jeffrey and Mary Archer. Grantchester Dene, formerly No. 2 Littledown Road, is now part of Dean Park Road, having been detached from its original street by an inner-relief road. Rupert wrote of it as 'Bournemouth, South of France' because its 'moaning pines' reminded him of the Riviera. Edwardian Lulworth was a more vibrant place, he wrote in letters, because it lacked 'decrepit and grey-haired invalids'.

But for the First World War he may have returned for Christmases and even retirement to his favourite place in Purbeck but there was a classical saying that he wished upon himself: 'Whom the gods love die young.'

1915

'The Oxen',
by Thomas Hardy

Christmas Eve, and twelve of the clock.
'Now they are all on their knees,'
An elder said as we sat in a flock
By the embers in the hearthside cease.

We pictured the meek mild creatures where
They dwelt in their strawy pen,
Nor did it occur to one of us there
To doubt they were kneeling then.

So fair a fancy few would weave
In these years! Yet, I feel,
If someone said on Christmas Eve,
'Come; see the oxen kneel

'In the lonely barton by yonder coomb,
Our childhood used to know,'
I should go with him in the gloom,
Hoping it might be so.

1923

Christmas Alone with Lawrence of Arabia

Going through one of the recurrent phases in his life of applied abstinence from contact with others, national hero Colonel Thomas Edward Lawrence turned down the offer of spending Christmas Day with Britain's internationally-famous novelist, Thomas Hardy, in 1923. Having enlisted as Private Shaw in the Tank Corps at Bovington Camp, and found as his retreat a gamekeeper's cottage secreted in the rhododendron clump a mile away on Clouds Hill, the enigmatic character known to the world as Lawrence of Arabia had 'Dorsetshire to look at'.

Having told his literary friend Sydney Cockerell that 'I'm no longer much company for real people' he disappeared when Ernest Altounyan, an Armenian, came down to see him. Altounyan found a boy who knew that Lawrence, in his words, drove at 'top-speed through these unfit

'Haute Cuisine': T.E. Lawrence at Clouds Hill, drawn by Eric Kennington.

roads' and pointed where 'Broughie' Shaw had gone. The Armenian heard that Lawrence was 'down by the river' and caught up with the diminutive man and his powerful Brough Superior motorcycle beside the South Bridge over the Frome at Wareham. Lawrence turned towards Altounyan, who was shocked at his reception:

As he approached I saw again that hunted look which I had last caught in Dover Street [London]. He was afraid for a moment that I was going to ask him where he had been. It was as though he mistrusted the felicity of the evening and could not quite believe my respect and understanding of his need for absolute freedom. I never realised so keenly as I did at that moment the utter loneliness of his life.

It was as though he had fallen into the habit (he who was so disdainful of all habits) of never expecting complete intimacy, however great the host of his devoted friends. 'I have never loved anyone,' he wrote to me once, 'or hardly ever. Lands and people – yes'; meaning that he had never experienced an affection which he felt to be undamaging to his or the other's freedom.

I said nothing, but after breakfast, getting up every particle of courage, I attacked, accusing him of cowardice in personal relationship. 'Don't retreat from me,' I said at last in despair. He looked at me dully and then asked me to come and see his motor bicycle. We never doubted each other again; but I saw now what he meant when he had said the night before: 'I haven't had much kick out of life; those days in Carchemish were the best.' By the merest accident of my own make-up I had stumbled on the truth. No one has ever lived so much alone.

Thomas and Florence Hardy knew that Lawrence would not be making any arrangements for Christmas and invited him to join them at their Max Gate home in Dorchester. Lawrence declined, as he explained to Sydney Cockerell: 'It is not good to be too happy often.'

Instead he did 'rations and coalyard' duty at Bovington so that others would be 'free for their orgy... Xmas means something to them. My pernickety mind discovers an incompatibility between their joint professions of Soldiers and Christians.' Then he returned to Clouds Hill and wrote to R.M. Guy: 'Xmas – spent alone in my new-old cottage – has been a quiet time of simply thinking.'

What the Hardys received was a more elaborate excuse. Lawrence wrote to Mrs Hardy on 22 December 1923:

> I wanted to see if I could and I'm afraid I can't. It's a good thing because it would feel intrusive to go to lunch on Christmas Day. However, I would probably have fallen to it, only that I'm without transport. The ancient and splendid bicycle was borrowed (without leave) by a villager who rode her ignorantly and left her, ruined, in a ditch. It saved me the pang of selling the poor beast, but also it shuts me unhealthily close to camp – and so I'm trying to persuade the maker of it to supply me another! I'll hope to see you and Mr Hardy soon.

Lawrence allowed himself to be persuaded to go to Max Gate for lunch on 30 December. George Bernard Shaw and his wife, Charlotte, were there as well. Lawrence stayed for the afternoon. 'Private Shaw meets Public Shaw,' G.B.S. joked.

'Tell me about Max Gate,' Robert Graves would ask him.

'I can't,' Lawrence replied, but he did. 'It is strange to pass from the noise and thoughtlessness of sergeants' company into a peace so secure that in it not even Mrs Hardy's teacups rattle on the tray; and from a barrack of hollow senseless bustle to the cheerful calm of T.H. thinking about life to two or three of us.'

Thomas Hardy was then eighty-three years old and Lawrence was almost half a century younger at thirty-five. It seemed to him that the Wessex novelist was still living in the Dorset of Napoleonic times. Those years, to Hardy, had been the real First World War:

> Then he is so far away. Napoleon is a real man to him and the county of Dorsetshire echoes that name everywhere in Hardy's ears. He lives in his period, and thinks of it as the great war; whereas to me that nightmare through the fringe of which I passed has dwarfed all memories of other wars, so that they seem trivial, half-amusing incidents.

Abstinence and Lawrence were synonymous in other ways. He was teetotal and his diet was somewhere between frugal and non-existent. 'Haute Cuisine' was how Eric Kennington depicted it, in a previously unpublished cartoon showing Lawrence with an empty can. Corporal Alex Dixon described the food at Clouds Hill as 'picnic meals' in which 'stuffed olives, salted almonds, and Heinz baked beans were regular features'. They would be washed down 'by T.E.'s own blend of China tea'. He 'always ate standing up by the end of the wide oak mantelshelf which had been fitted at a height convenient for him'. It is this, at an obviously low height, which features in Kennington's cartoon.

Christmas would hardly have been much different, though F.J. Stratton, the Bovington butcher with a shop opposite the Post Office, insisted that he regularly bought 'two chops for his lunch'. The fishmongers, Mr and Mrs White, said he was partial 'to fish and chips and finnan haddock' but that if there was anyone else in the shop he would leave rather than queue. The problem with people took precedence over food.

Christmas post: arriving at Max Gate for Florence and Thomas Hardy in their greetings card of 1926 (also featuring 'the famous dog Wessex' whose most notable bite was out of author John Galsworthy).

1924

'Christmas',
by Thomas Hardy

'Peace upon Earth!' was said. We sing it,
And pay a million priests to bring it.
After two thousand years of mass
We've got as far as poison-gas.

Benjamin Pond Meets the Ghost of Curlew Cottage

It was in midwinter, Poole Harbour boatman Benjamin Pond told me, that he had his frightening encounter with the supernatural. He had been carrying out his pre-Christmas family visits, taking a train up the Somerset and Dorset line to visit a cousin in Blandford, and returning to Poole with a heavy package of books. There were no buses in those days at that time of the year or hour of the day so he had to walk the two miles to Sandbanks where he had moored his boat. He rowed across to Shell Bay. 'South Haven we always called it,' nautically and correctly, Ben pointed out.

> I'd no fear of the dark I can tell 'ee. I would walk across the whole of the heath on many a dark night and through many a dense plantation. My little shack was another 4 miles across the heath. Dark clouds had spread across the Purbeck sky and it was even darker along the track through the tall heather.

He had gone almost a mile when heavy drops of water fell from the black clouds. There had been a drastic change in temperature and a thunder-storm threatened. His immediate thoughts were to reach shelter. The location was on the sandy western side of Little Sea in the centre of wild heathland between Redhorn Quay and Brand's Ford. Both were empty places with names rather than habitation. 'I would normally have put up with getting wet,' he said, 'but I didn't want to risk my books and some rather nice eatables. The answer was to shelter in Curlew Cottages.'

These have long been gone from what is now a featureless spot at Ordnance Survey map reference SZ 026 851 in the northern arm of Studland Heath National Nature Reserve.

They had last been occupied, until seven years earlier, by the Wild Man who had disappeared at the end of the Great War. Ben Pond was regarded as his natural successor and was known as Wild Man Number Two. Both adopted a free-style Bohemian existence of beachcombing, fishing, boating and smuggling – allegedly or unwittingly – plus an artistic side to add to the romance. They were Purbeck's answer to Augustus John at Alderney Manor on the other side of Poole.

The original Wild Man had lived with the Crees, a Red Indian tribe on the Canadian side of the border, and his realistic life-size murals of Indian life, drawn in pastel colours on all the walls, still decorated Curlew Cottages. Ben had called there in daylight to admire them.

The cottages had long before been merged into one dwelling now engulfed in scrub. There was no front door. Ben sat down in a corner, on bare boards, as simultaneous flashes of lightning and claps of thunder showed that the storm was directly overhead. It illuminated the fierce eyes of an Indian chief, depicted in perfect detail, staring directly at Ben. Further along the wall there were wigwams, a dying fire, tall trees and a backdrop of the snow-covered Rocky Mountains.

Ben moved to another corner to try to avoid the penetrating eyes. They followed him. The chief was smiling and Ben sensed that he was enjoying the experience as boughs of trees and bushes lashed the walls and windows. His lips appeared to be moving.

Benjamin Pond had crossed the heath and found this refuge without a thought of apprehension beyond concern for protecting his books. Now he was shivering with absolute fear. There was a thud immediately above, in the upstairs room, followed by a second heavy thud. Ben was now sweating in absolute terror.

He dashed for freedom into the storm, his clothes being torn by brambles and gorse bushes, with the books and shopping scattered and abandoned where they fell. He ran until he reached the safety of his shack.

The following morning he returned to South Haven to take his boat back to Sandbanks. Mr Smith, the ferryman, told him: 'Tramp bloke, the Wild Man, is back. Bin away over seven years and bin back at Curlew a week. Already owes for two crossings.'

Wild Man Number Two met the genuine Wild Man later in the week. They exchanged their ghost stories. Each had spooked the other. Both had run for their lives. The returnee to Curlew Cottages was first to realise there had been a human intruder, when he found books and bags of food; 'Beachcombing on me doorstep, as you might say.' It had been the Wild Man's heavy boots on the bedroom floor.

Ben Pond bought him a replacement pair of the lightest type available, in Wareham, and smuggled them into the cottage when the Wild Man was at large. He left them upstairs beside a bed of heather. On the way out he glanced at the Indian chief; 'Was it a smile, or a look of contempt? I really wouldn't like to say.'

The Saving of the Bloxworth Carols

The best old-style English country carols, together with the tradition of singing them each Christmas in St Andrew's parish church at Bloxworth, owe their survival to the efforts of William Adair Pickard-Cambridge (1879–1957). He was the son of the Victorian rector, 'Spider Man' Rev. Octavius Pickard-Cambridge (1828–1927), who became the first national authority on Britain's arachnid fauna and was the last of the great naturalist parsons. He discovered and gave the village name to the Bloxworth Snout Moth which was rare in both Victorian and modern Bloxworth but is now said to be common in the wartime German bunkers on Guernsey.

Eight local carols had been recorded at Bloxworth by John Skinner of Buttlands, the parish clerk for sixty-two years, from 1817 to 1879. He set them out with words and music. These and other Dorset versions were sung, in the main, to the 'Old Methodist' type of tune which had passed out of fashion and was no longer found in print. Pickard-Cambridge gathered another 33 examples for *A Collection of Dorset Carols* which he published in 1926. Three are attributed to Samuel Wakely who used to visit the Mellstock Quire, Thomas Hardy recalled, with 'tunes of his own composure' which inspired his poem 'The Paphian Ball'.

By this time, such bands were regarded as 'too noisy' for churches and even at Bloxworth the residual Christmas

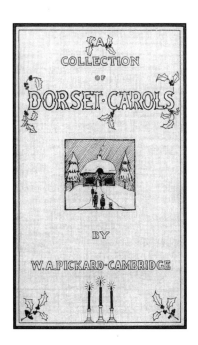

music had gone underground – or at least sideways – first into the drawing-room of the Rectory, and then the schoolroom during the First World War. Between the wars the carol service progressed to the Memorial Hall, which had been built by Mr and Mrs Frederick Lane of Bloxworth House, in memory of their two sons who fell in the First World War. Music then returned to St Andrew's where 'carolling' has gone on ever since the Second World War, except during the hiatus following William Pickard-Cambridge's death in 1957. Colonel Lane intervened to ensure that the tradition resumed. He also ensured its popularity by transferring the annual service from January to 15.00 hours on the Sunday before Christmas.

An Oxford scholar and classics lecturer, Pickard-Cambridge also translated Aristotle, in particular the Topics and Sophistici Elenchi in 1928. He was an accomplished organist who, on retirement to Brimlands in Water Tower Road at Broadstone, became conductor of the Madrigal Group of the Bournemouth Chamber Music Group in 1950, and produced many original songs and motets.

Many of the Christmas carols were recorded from several locations, such as 'Behold what news we bring' (no. 29) which came from both Bloxworth and Worth Matravers. 'Blessed are the sons of Peace' (no. 11) came from all over Dorset, from Hazelbury Bryan and Mappowder in the Blackmore Vale, to the Piddle Valley and Worth on the Purbeck coast. 'See seraphic throngs descending' (no. 33) was also particularly popular, with versions from Worth Matravers, Morden, Bloxworth, Puddletown and Hazelbury Bryan. 'Wrapt in the silence of the night' (no. 36) had a similar distribution. Unfortunately the names of the singers and informants are not given so the Worth contact remains anonymous. He may well have been quarryman William Jeremiah Bower, known as 'Billy Winspit', who certainly played them on his fiddle at the Square and Compass and entertained Bohemian artist Augustus John and his entourage.

Where there were only minor differences in the text or tune, Pickard-Cambridge reconciled them into what is now the definitive Dorset version. On the other hand, when they existed with totally different tunes, he had to choose what he considered to be the best version. With 'While shepherds were feeding their flocks in the field' (no. 2) he decided that two tunes had equal merit, and gives both. The common version came from Bloxworth and Morden in the Purbeck hinterland, and Stratton from beyond Dorchester. Its alternative tune was found in Winterborne Zelston, between Bere Regis and Charborough Park.

The words of the carols are now regarded as a pocket of history but they are of dubious antiquity. Most can be traced to eighteenth- and nineteenth-century broadsheets and national authors such as Nahum Tate, Isaac Watts and Alexander Pope. One of these printed versions admitted – with rare honesty verging upon commercial suicide – that a particular song was tired and 'will at no distant period become obsolete'. There was also a difficulty in deciding upon the 'correct versions' as 'no one who is familiar with either the old broadsheets or the human memory will be surprised if not infrequently a verse or half-verse of one carol pitches its tent in the middle of another'.

Editing was particularly necessary when it came to the tunes. Not only were many extinct, even in non-conformist hymn books, but their rendition was patchy and unconvincing. 'In some cases the extreme corruption, in others the relative dullness, of the harmonies as written in the manuscripts have compelled me to re-write rather freely,' Pickard-Cambridge confesses, 'but the result preserves, I hope, the spirit.' This, to quote from one of the carols, was 'the joy and pious mirth' characteristic of old country carollings. 'How wide a range of religious feeling that spirit includes will be evident to anyone who peruses the carols themselves.'

Pickard-Cambridge points out that their origins are non-evangelical, and a far cry from the exuberant black slave music that was then evolving into jazz, with only occasional exceptions:

> If cheerfulness and a lively alertness are the prevailing moods that is what should be – but the carols are ill-performed if such moods, however exultant, are ever made to appear lacking in their appropriate restraint. Nor do they exclude – they merely set off – moods of sublime dignity and devout tenderness. May this edition help both to deepen and to widen the appreciation of the singularly healthy and I believe peculiarly English attitude towards Christmas and its story which the carols express.

While shepherds were feeding their flocks in the field

(First tune) "KING STREET." John Moreton, Birmingham, (1764-1804)

Allegretto. (♩ =66)

mf While Shep-herds were feed-ing their flocks in the field, The birth of our Sa-viour to them was re-vealed; And An-gels as-sem-bling in clouds did ap-pear While Shep-herds lay tremb-ling and smit-ten with fear. *f* While Shep-herds lay tremb-ling and smit-ten with fear.

While shepherds were feeding their flocks in the field

(Second tune)

Andante. (♩=80)

mf While Shep-herds were feed-ing their flocks in the field, The
birth of our Sa - viour to them was re-vealed; And An - gels as
semb - ling in clouds did ap - pear While Shep - herds lay
trembling, While Shep-herds lay trembling and smit-ten with fear.

2.

f Forbear to be fearful, you've reason to sing:
Rejoice and be cheerful, glad tidings I bring;
There's born in the City of David therefore
A Saviour of pity, whom all will adore.

3.

f He's come to redeem us from guilt and from sin: [begin.
For love He would have you new lives to
In love each believer shall gladly adore
For ever and ever, when time is no more.

N.B. The expression should be the same in each verse, as marked in the music.

Behold what news we bring

2.

mf At Bethlehem arriv'd,
They sought him in the morn ;
And there they found the holy place,
Where Jesus Christ was born.

3.

f All glory be to God,
Who doth His favour show !
Goodwill be unto all mankind,
p And peace on earth below !

[*N.B The last line but one of each verse should be sung,
1st time p, 2nd time cres., last time f, as in verse 1.*]

Thomas Hardy's last Christmastide

The rain-shafts splintered on me
As despondently I strode;
The twilight gloomed upon me
And bleared the blank high-road.
Each bush gave forth, when blown on
By gusts in shower and shower,
A sigh, as it were sown on
In handfuls by a sower.

A cheerful voice called, nigh me,
'A merry Christmas, friend!' –
There rose a figure by me,
Walking with townward trend,
A sodden tramp's, who, breaking
Into thin song, bore straight
Ahead, direction taking
Toward the Casual's gate.

1943

'Black Christmas' at Tyneham

The last Christmas for Tyneham villagers took place in 1942 though no one knew it at the time. Their following Christmas would have to be spent in a variety of emergency accommodation following the diaspora of 19 December 1943 in which more than 10 square miles were depopulated. This was to enable an extension of the Lulworth Ranges for live-firing Sherman tanks of the Allied armies that would fight the Battle of Normandy in the months after D-Day.

All this was top secret – or 'most secret' as the British bureaucracy worded it – on the direct orders of Winston Churchill's War Cabinet. No local consultation was allowed, not even with councils or committees, and nothing was printed in the

Displaced person: John Gould lost his home at Tyneham on 19 December 1943, while he was fighting overseas with the British Army in India.

press beyond a succession of auction notices for the stock and equipment of what were termed 'quitting' farmers. Their departure from the land was compulsory, in the wake of requisition notices, as Purbeck's spectacular western coastline and its hinterland received the following pledge:

This means that when the War Department has no further use for the property and it is handed back, you have every right to return to the property. It should not be assumed that because the War Department has turned you out, you lose your right of occupying the premises again.

The Second World War had already visited Tyneham and Worbarrow Bay. Estate landowner Ralph Bond commanded its Home Guard platoon. Defence Area restrictions applied to a mined Worbarrow Bay. The Bond family's Elizabethan mansion of Tyneham House had already been occupied by the military as staff quarters for a coastal radar station, above Egliston Gwyle, that was designated RAF Brandy Bay. Many local people, including just about all the young men who were not in reserve occupations, had gone off to war. Mail censorship would prevent them being told why their parents were moving.

Military users, second-home holiday cottagers, and a host of Purbeck farmers and fishermen and their labourers are listed as the occupiers of 106 properties served with clearance orders in November 1943. The operation started with military logic, beside the sea, and then spread inland up the valley and across the Purbeck Hills. Many of the buildings had no name beyond that of their tenants. 'The postman found us by our name,' one of them told me. It is a poignant document that gave them what would be remembered as 'Black Christmas':

1. Worbarrow (Thomas Miller)
2. Worbarrow (Charles Miller, boatman)
2a. Worbarrow (also Charles Miller)
3. Worbarrow (Jack Miller)
4. Worbarrow (Miss Beatrice A. Mintern and Miss Winifred E. Mintern)
5. Sheepleaze, Worbarrow (Philip Draper of Silver Birches, Brook, Albury, Surrey)
6. Bungalow, Worbarrow (Squadron Leader C.C. Brachi, Knoll House, Bourne End, Boxmoor, Hertfordshire)
7. Baltington Farm (Albert B. Longman)
8. Baltington Farm Cottages (Mr and Mrs Kerley)
8a. Baltington Farm outbuilding (Empty)
9. The Laundry, Tyneham (William Taylor)
10. Parish Church, Tyneham (Rev. Humphrey Churchill Money, Royal Engineers, Officers' Mess, Pickwick Villas, Corsham, Wiltshire)

11. The Row, Tyneham (Empty)
12. Post Office, Tyneham (Mrs Gwendoline Driscoll)
13. Farm Cottage, Tyneham (Empty)
14. Gwyle Cottage, Tyneham (Part, empty)
15. Gwyle Cottage, Tyneham (Part, already requisitioned)
16. School Cottage, Tyneham (NAAFI, catering for men and women of RAF Brandy Bay; see 20 for their relaxation room)
17. The Rectory, Tyneham (Already requisitioned)
18. Rectory Cottage, Tyneham (Already requisitioned)
19. School Building, Tyneham (Already requisitioned)
20. Parish Hut, Tyneham (NAAFI)
21. Gardener's Cottage, Tyneham (Thomas Gould)
22. The Cottage, Tyneham (Dudley Coles)
23. The Cottage, Tyneham (George Everett)
24. Museum Cottage, Tyneham (Ralph Bond)
25. Tyneham House (Royal Air Force, as offices and quarters for RAF Brandy Bay)
26. Tyneham Farm (S.C. Churchill)
27. Dairy House, Tyneham Farm (Mrs Taylor)
28. Undescribed property, Worbarrow (Empty)
29. Cottage and garden, Worbarrow (Reg Ware)
30. Boathouses, Worbarrow (Ralph Bond)
31. Boathouses, Worbarrow (Philip Draper)
32. North Egliston Farm (Herbert John House)
33. Farm Cottages, North Egliston (Arthur House)
34. Chapel Cottage, North Egliston (Mr Bradford)
35. Lutton Farm (Albert Ernest Cranton)
36. Farm Cottage (Arthur Stockley)
37. Farm Cottage, Lutton (William Smith)
38. Farm Cottage, Lutton (Mrs Mitchell)
39. South Tyneham Cottage (Lieutenant-Commander Godfrey E.H. House RN, Royal Navy Barracks, Portsmouth)
40. South Tyneham Cottage (Mrs Rose)
41. South Egliston (Mrs Bartholomew, Rimpton House, Yeovil, Somerset; sub-tenant of the Misses L.C.T. Bond and L.S. Bond who were tenants for life under the will trust of Walter Bond)
42. Stickland's Cottage, near Kimmeridge Bay (William Stickland)
43. Black Cottage, near Kimmeridge Bay (C.M. Robinson)
44. King Cottage, near Kimmeridge Bay (A.R. Wills, Oslease, Belbins, Romsey, Hampshire)
45. Boathouse, Charnel, Kimmeridge Bay (William Stickland)
46. 66 West Whiteway Cottages, Povington (J. Askew)
47. 67 West Whiteway Cottages, Povington (C. Wells)
48. West Whiteway Farm, Povington (I. H. Sampson)
49. 64 West Whiteway Cottages, Povington (G. Burt)
50. 65 West Whiteway Cottages, Povington (G. Plant)

51.   Farwell's Holding, Povington (Mrs Mawas)

52.   Searley's Living, Povington (Arthur Cooper)

53.   Povington Farm Cottage (Empty, with G. Cooper being away on active service)

54.   Victoria Cottage, Povington (F.C. Cross, agricultural sub-tenant for T.W. Wrixon)

55.   Heather Cottage, Povington Farm (Mr Glandfield, 24 Avenue Gardens, Teddington, Middlesex)

56.   Heath Cottage, Povington Farm (R.J. Way, who also cultivates the garden of Heather Cottage)

57.   Cottage, Povington (F.H. Cleall)

58.   Primrose Cottage, Povington Farm (Miss Allday, Cornelia Hospital, Poole)

59.   Cottage, Povington (W.J. Cooper)

60.   Pine Tree Cottage (Mrs Singleton)

61.   Povington Farm, Povington (Thomas Walter Wrixon)

62.   Cottage, Povington (C. Goff)

63.   Jiggiting Corner, Povington (J. Cooper)

64.   Batty Corner Farm, Povington (F.P. Cooper)

65.   Rookery Farm, Povington (F. Cranton)

66.   Orchard Cottages, Povington (P. Taylor, a serving military tenant)

67.   Orchard Cottages, Povington (H. Toms, an estate pensioner receiving 5 shillings a week)

68.   West Creech Farm (R.J. Cake)

69.   West Creech Farm (C.W. James, a serving military tenant)

70.   West Creech Farm (Mrs H.K. Saxton)

71.   Broadmoor Farm, West Creech (Robert Green)

72.   Hollow Ditch, West Creech (Mrs Charles)

73.   Whitehall Farm, West Creech (William Cake)

74.   Taylor's Cottage, West Creech (Harold Gover)

75.   Keeper's Cottage, West Creech (S. Dorey)

76.   Oak Tree Cottage, West Creech (Albert Taylor)

77.   Oak Tree Cottage, West Creech (Robert Charles)

78.   Hurst Mill Farm (E. Swain)

79.   Bridewell Cottages (F.W. Norris)

80.   Bridewell Cottages (Mr Osborne)

81.   Bridewell Cottages (Sergeant Lucas)

82.   Taken out of area (Reprieved from requisition)

83.   Taken out of area (Reprieved from requisition)

84.   New Barn Cottages (H.T. Newbery)

85.   New Barn Cottages (W.J.G. Trent)

86.   No. 1 West Holme Cottages (Mr Collins)

87.   No. 2 West Holme Cottages (George Marshallsay)

88.   No. 3 West Holme Cottages (Ernest Barnes)

89.   The Poplars (P. Pearce junior, 38 Roxeth Hill, Harrow, Middlesex)

90.   The Cat, 63 Wareham Road (W.D. Damen, 543 Wareham Road, East Lulworth)

91.   Wareham Lodge (E.A.F. Stockley)

92.   'Heatherway' Caravan (A.V. Robinson, Beehive Cottage, Holme Bridge, East Stoke)

93.   Land at South Tyneham (Tom Hooper, Newburgh Farm, Winfrith)

94. Hut at Charnel, beside Kimmeridge Bay (Mrs Bartholomew)
95. Heathland at West Holme Heath (Colonel E. Eaton, Spur Hill, Folkestone)
96. Farmland adjacent to Weld Arms Inn, East Lulworth (Edwin Bonham)
97. Meadow (R.J. Champ, Littlemore Cottage, East Lulworth)
98. Lands in hand (Lulworth Castle Estate)
99. Ferny Barrows, East Lulworth (Edwin Bonham, Weld Arms Inn)
100. Lands in hand (John Wentworth Garneys Bond, Creech Grange)
101. Lands in hand (D.N.H. Bond)
102. Part of West Holme Lodge Farm, East Stoke (Mrs M.A. Chilcott)
103. Part of Holme Farm, East Holme (Alan H. Barnes)
104. Lands in hand (Lieutenant-Colonel Ashley Bond)
105. Part of Botany Farm, East Lulworth (Executors of Herbert George Crocker deceased, and H.J. Crocker)
106. Part of Home Farm, East Lulworth (F.G. White, G.B. White and K.W. White)

They pinned a poignant notice to the door of St Mary's parish church:

> Please treat the church and houses with care; we have given up our homes where many of us lived for generations to help win the war to keep men free. We shall return one day and thank you for treating the village kindly.

One of the ironies of the non-return of Tyneham to its former villagers is that its current opening arrangements make it one of the busiest outdoor attractions in the Isle of Purbeck on Christmas Day. The surrounding network of coastal paths, the Lulworth Range Walks, are also open most weekends and during Army block-leave periods at Easter and through the month of August. It has become a time-warp landscape of antiquities and wildlife in a natural wilderness that flourishes on a scale unprecedented on the South Coast.

I called it 'Redgrave Park' in tribute to Brigadier Redgrave, Commandant of the Royal Armoured Corps. Writing his memoirs in 2000, as Sir Roy Redgrave, he remembered this in *Balkan Blue* and said he was delighted that as 'a constant critic of the Army', I had been 'generous enough' to coin the phrase, and quoted from my magazine editorial:

The virtual conversion of a major Army range from a weekday training ground into a weekend public park has been mastermined by Brigadier Redgrave. He has coped successfully with balancing traditional military activities with new mass access plans. Redgrave, who deserves 'Public Relations Officer of the Year' for this achievement, leaves Bovington in November.

Sir Roy goes on to make it clear how much he enjoyed Tyneham and Purbeck, at a time when the Cold War was continuing, and he found himself bound for 'the ugly wall' inside the Iron Curtain:

And so it was to be. All good things had to come to an end but I was taken completely by surprise to be told that my next posting was to be to that stimulating and exciting city, Berlin.

Tyneham House: already occupied by the military when this photograph was taken in the autumn of 1943, it too would be emptied.

1969

Winter of the Twitchers

The Christmas of the twitchers was that of 1969. At that time birders were called 'tick-hunters' because of their obsessive ticking of species in their ornithological check-list. Once they have gone through those in the British national list they move on to strays from overseas that are occasionally blown off course and across thousands of miles of ocean. Such specimens usually make their landfall in inhospitable places and many are exhausted and expire before the network of twitchers hears of their presence.

One visitor, however, led an almost charmed life. The North American wallcreeper that arrived at Winspit in November 1969 was the first that had been seen in the British Isles since 1938. Not only did it fail to expire but it decided to stay on the stone cliffs. By Christmas the Square and Compass was under a state of siege and hundreds of bird-watchers surged down the valley from Worth Matravers to the rocky cliffs between Seacombe and St Alban's Head. It was before the era of the Barbour and they looked more like bikers as they were dressed in black leathers. Arriving in the old quarries they paired off, almost in a mating ritual, with each couple taking possession of their chosen spot behind a rock where they would stay motionless for hours. They bristled with binoculars, telephoto lenses and telescopes.

It would be wrong to call them ornithologists because they showed no interest in any bird other than the wallcreeper. No one broke ranks to observe the sea birds, or would be distracted by an offshore peregrine falcon, except in the hope that it might have the wallcreeper in its talons. The objective was to see the wallcreeper and depart. Colin Graham and I joined them and failed utterly. We lacked the necessary single-issue determination and found ourselves looking at other things and people. They were worthy of study. Some exhibited distinct signs of psychosis. One wondered where they were from, what they did between birds, and what motivated their strange patterns of behaviour. 'We don't have them in the States,' we were reassured by a non-birding American visitor who seemed unaccustomed to taking the mental high ground.

Some of the twitchers came to grief. One departed with a broken leg and failed to gather the coveted tick for his list. The crowd over the Christmas holiday made enough distur-bance to drive every bird from the county, except the wallcreeper which must have come to think that all this attention was NFD – 'Normal for Dorset' – and stayed for months. It was still around at Easter and held its alien territory until the influx of swallows and other spring migrants. Avian rather than human disturbance caused it to head for where we know not. The last sighting was in April 1970.

'That bird could write a book,' Helen Brotherton told me.

North Street, Wareham, when the snow of 9 March 1891 blocked all roads across Dorset.

1978

The Great Snow

An earlier blizzard. The road from Kingston to Langton Matravers, in 1924, looking eastwards from the 'Wareham 8' milestone with a stone working to the left and the Acton turning on the right, signed to Worth Matravers and St Alban's Head.

The last great winter of the twentieth century, before anyone talked of global warming, brought a phenomenal snowfall in February 1978. Moderate snow just after the middle of the month, on Thursday and Friday (16–17 February), was followed by heavy snow and strong winds on Saturday, 18 February which made most roads in Dorset impassable by late evening. People were being stranded all over the county, particularly around the county town, and at the request of the police, Coburg Road School, Dorchester, was opened as an emergency rest centre.

Professor Bryan N. Brooke, a surgeon at St James's Hospital, Balham, was spending the weekend at his Purbeck retreat in Worth Matravers. In the afternoon the frost in the top couple of inches of soil enabled him to lift his leaks, cleanly, for the first time in months as a strong wind blew from the southeast:

> While I dug, it swung further to the east and increased in strength. Now I could only stand with difficulty. It blew harder, reaching

Slushy road to the bay at Kimmeridge.

Force Nine to Ten, and howling over the roof and chimneys of the house. As darkness fell, fine drops of snow sped horizontally, stinging my face as I moved into the house to warm up by the welcoming Aga. The chimney flue had meanwhile swung through the full right angle to lie horizontally; a useful anemometer.

Ilay arrived at seven-thirty and was the first of our guests for dinner. He was drenched with snow after walking the odd mile in the wind from his hut in the quarry by the road to St Alban's Head. I found him a dry pair of pants and poked my nose out of the door. The glistening white particles were rushing overhead, some passing out of sight but others being caught by circular eddies into a feverish fandango. Our other three guests telephoned to cry off.

After dinner we tried to persuade Ilay to stay the night. His independence demanded otherwise, with the excuse that he wanted to keep his stove going. He set out on foot, but within half an hour he was back – beaten by a drift half a mile away at the Dutch barns.

In any persistent southwesterly gale the electric power here gives out. Easterlies were to prove no exception. The lights flicked out then on for the usual six times – and then permanent darkness. A torchlight check of the east-facing door revealed snow now accumulating in the porch. Inspection of all east windows in the house and cottage showed the snow pouring through the smallest chink of what appeared to be close fittings. A drift lay in the cottage sitting room, against the door. That was dug out and swept up. And so to bed, after caulking all hatches with paper.

The wind howled unabated the next morning, the Aga anemometer still registering the horizontal full force. Outside the open fields and our lawn were almost bare but snow had drifted around every wall, hedge, building and other obstruction. It grew into long wide masses rising to ten feet or more. Strange and beautiful forms were part sculptural, part architectural.

A sunken drive between two walls was filled with snow except for a passageway against the western wall. Here the impact of the wind had caused an updraught, leaving almost a tunnel with finely curved walls and a roof, actually growing as you looked. A white precipice rose hourly up the kitchen windows until even the tower of Worth Matravers church was obscured from view.

Together with grandchildren, we sallied forth to savour the mysteries of the transient scenes. We were soon to return, however, discouraged by the force of the wind and snow. It penetrated the most protective garments. News – local information – became a compelling need. So, to the pub, after plunging through deep snow wherever a passage looked possible. The technique was to lean forward against the wind, slit-eyed against the stinging white particles, as they swirled off the head of each drift.

The Square and Compass had become a proper 'local'. There were none of the usual Sunday morning foreigners filling the pub to the exclusion of the villagers. Instead of subdued voices, and personal chat in private groups, conversation today was joined by all. Acquaintance was rediscovered in the close confines of the tap-room under the duress of disruption and the excitement it was creating plus warming whisky-macs. Experiences were exchanged. We learnt that the Auxiliary Coastguard on night watch in the little exposed hut on the Head, a retired marine of sixty-one, could not be relieved at the end of his watch and had spent fifteen hours alone on constant lookout until daylight came. After that the station had to be abandoned.

Early collection: '6.30 am' being the given time on the letterbox beside a classic K6 telephone kiosk at Old Bond Street, Creech.

The elderly in the village were identified and discussed. I was able to report that George, living alone in a squalid wood hut two drifts away from me, seemed unconcerned. Communication was difficult, through his deafness, but his only vexation lay outside – not in the storm but the fact that the cover to a septic tank beside the door of his hovel had been blown off.

The farm was in trouble. Some of the herd was lost in the snow on the Head and there was no chance of storing milk until the tankers could get through again. It would have to be poured away. Some of us downed our drinks smartly, made tracks for the dairy, and saved a few pints for ourselves.

Main road, between the pines at Norden, after a gentle snowfall.

At the dairy we were told that water had ceased to flow to the village. The pumps to lift it over the hill, from the reservoir in the valley, had stopped with the power failure. Back to the house, as quickly as possible against the forceful gusts, and into the attic. The cold water tank had only six inches left. Immediately siege discipline was applied – no plugs were pulled, or taps turned.

Out into the drifts, to scoop up snow in every available bucket and bin to place them by the Aga, though we discovered that snow is reluctant to melt, except when directly heated in the kettle. The buckets and bins yielded little, if any, water by breakfast next morning.

The county-wide picture between midnight and dawn on Sunday 19 February was that blizzard conditions had intensified. Fine freeze-dried snow, driven by a wind from Siberia, defeated all attempts at clearing roads. Reports continued of people stranded, and others missing, and by 10.00 hours a Control Centre was operational at Police Divisional Headquarters, Weymouth Avenue, Dorchester. A county-wide check began and blankets were provided to those in need in the few places where movement was still possible. Whole towns were cut off and the only lifeline into the county was the railway from Bournemouth and Poole through to Weymouth. Its counterpart in the north, the line from Waterloo to Exeter via Gillingham and Sherborne, passed through the epicentre of the blizzard and was consequently blocked.

Corfe Castle preparing for Christmas, seen from East Hill.

As for the southern route, it was just about usable in slow motion, and an attempt was made to reach Weymouth from Dorchester. By 16.00 hours, however, this was reported to be stuck in Bincombe cutting on the side of Ridgeway Hill. Plans were put in hand to rescue its hundred passengers but in the event it managed to reach Weymouth eventually. In the other direction, from Dorchester, a packed train managed to reach Poole and Bournemouth, but could not escape from the county as drifts blocked miles of line in the New Forest.

No movement of homeless or displaced people was possible on Monday, 20 February. All roads remained closed and the sole emergency service across more than a thousand square miles was provided by Royal Navy helicopters from Yeovilton and Portland. These carried out life-saving operations to check out abandoned cars and delivered fodder to the fields for farmers. Humans were assumed to have food for a few days but there were now fears that the cold might last longer. George Baynes, the Emergency Officer for Dorset County Council based in the Cold War bunker beneath the County Library in Colliton Park, Dorchester, made arrangements for stores to be released by a wholesale supplier in Dorchester, and for bread to be baked in Weymouth.

Bryan Brooke, still snowed-in and alternating between his house and the Square and Compass, was planning his next expedition at Worth Matravers:

With no snow falling now and the wind, though strong, abating, we trekked to the village shop to replace stocks of paraffin and candles, and to meet the other inhabitants of our isolated little world. Behind the grill which serves as a post office at the end of the shop, the telephone rang. Peter, the shopkeeper, announced to those determined on tramping 3 to 5 miles over the hill – to obtain bread in Langton or Swanage – that there was no point. The bakeries, too, had been forced into inactivity by the power and water failures. We suppressed our sense of complacent self-satisfaction at the thought of the dough at that moment rising on the top of our stove. Instead we offered Peter the hospitality of our oven to cook the turkeys that were rapidly thawing in the shop's deep-freeze.

Phones at our end of the village had failed. So while in the shop I made urgent calls to my hospital to warn that I might not be able to get away in time to be in London for an operation on Wednesday. I also put my problem to the police in Swanage – only to be told that all roads out of Purbeck were closed. Then it was back through the snowy ramparts to the Square and Compass.

There was more than the usual consolation, as two Coastguards obligingly suggested a helicopter as a solution. It might even get me to what had now become the railhead, Portsmouth or Southampton. Elated at the prospect of a new experience, I ordered further drinks all round and leaving the pub took a turn at pulling the improvised sleigh, a galvanised bath-tub. It was being dragged with ropes by friends to carry provisions to their isolated domain over a mile away.

Later there was a message from the Coastguards, who had put their radio to use on my account, that I was to ring their base at Weymouth. I walked back to the village to find an active phone, but was referred politely to the police at Dorchester, who suggested that the chief inspector at Wareham was my man.

Even had they offered, there was nothing that could have been done through Portland Heliport, as the weather added a new problem. On Tuesday, 21 February thick fog grounded the helicopters. Just one machine attempted an emergency mission, trying to take a medical team to Piddlehinton, but had to return to base after an exceedingly hazardous flight. Police and emergency officers held a crisis meeting with representatives of Wessex Water Authority, Southern Electricity Board, Wessex Health Authority, the Armed Forces and the National Farmers' Union. The first reports came in of places and institutions running out of provisions. Milton Abbey School requested a helicopter-drop

Snug thatch in West Street at Corfe Castle.

though its supplies were taken across the downs by an Army tracked vehicle from Bovington. Five families in temporary accommodation at Piddlehinton Camp were reported to be in desperate need and efforts were made to secure them credit at the village stores. Abbotsbury village had no bread and its emergency supply was stacked on the tarmac at Portland Heliport awaiting the lifting of the fog. Villagers had to look after themselves and did so by walking over the fields to collect their loaves from caravan country near Weymouth.

Everywhere, walking was the only solution, but over the land rather than along lanes as there 'the snow was so deep you could sit on top of the telegraph poles'. Most of the snow had blown off the fields and drifted between roadside hedges and banks. Social workers and carers made most of their visits to the elderly and vulnerable on foot. Meals on wheels became food on the hoof where vehicular access was impossible.

In Worth Matravers, Bryan Brooke tried to phone Wareham police, but found yet more telephones were dead. Engineers explained that the batteries in the sub-exchange uphill from the Square and Compass had run low and that subscribers were being cut-off to lessen the load:

> Nothing could be done until generators were brought through. Concern was also growing for the farmer and his herd, which needed two thousand gallons of water each day – and the birds likewise were deprived of drinking water. For the latter, dishes were placed outside the back door. The cows were offered their own milk, which they regarded with distaste. Meanwhile our local grapevine, Radio Solent, gave hope that electricity might be restored.

> Somewhere out there were engineers braving the rigours to mend our lines, as momentary flickers of light confirmed. But hopes were dashed regarding transport, for no trains could get beyond Southampton. There followed ten minutes or more of lists of schools in the area which were closed, the wonder being that there were so many to close. 'What's off' was followed by listings of events.

In the evening there was more than a flicker – for several minutes twentieth-century light outshone kerosene lamp and candle, which we proceeded to extinguish with a peculiar sense of guilt. Guilt or relief; three days without modern power had raised questions in the mind as to the propriety of the convenience in the face of the elements, even the right to such luxury. Just to remind us of our dependence, a remote distant influence cast us again into outer darkness. But as we fumbled for matches, mysteriously and arbitrarily our luxury was again restored. We listened for the cascade of a cistern filling in the loft but six hours were to pass before siege discipline could be relaxed – for downhill from us those two thousand gallons were being absorbed to succour cows.

On Wednesday, 22 February the previous day's crisis conference was reconvened, and was joined by Dennis Howell, the Government minister overseeing emergency operations. Piddlehinton remained a weak link among the villages, having now run out of food, and the Army promised to reach it with a tracked vehicle. Stores were delivered to the post office and a social worker took money and food to the distressed families at Piddlehinton Camp.

Bryan Brooke resumes the story of what becomes his escape from Worth Matravers:

The phone was still out of action on Wednesday so I tried elsewhere, noting on the way the dense mist of the thaw, and finding a council bulldozer had broken through to raise the siege. The road from Wareham had just been opened and the railhead had reached the station there. The police voice confirmed news from Radio Solent of restrictions placed by the law upon movement by road – only for emergencies and then in four-wheel drive.

On the way back to the house the two Coastguards appeared out of the misty gloom in their official Land Rover, off to find a road open and get petrol if they could. There was some doubt about the outcome since the tanker-drivers' strike, which had preceded the blizzard, had caused garages to close. They promised to return shortly and take me out if all went well.

The next hour was spent attacking drifts in the drive, a seemingly Herculean task as a preliminary to releasing cars, made easier by cutting blocks as though to build an igloo. The Coastguard rescue vehicle arrived and our journey progressed circuitously through high white cliffs cut by bulldozers and fork-lifts. A single track was open on the road from Swanage. There the traffic was beginning to move. We eventually left the Isle of Purbeck at the bridge over the river in Wareham, where a police road-block was turning back everyone except those claiming to be carrying out an essential task. The distinctive rescue markings of the Coastguard Land Rover were an instant passport for access into the beleaguered town. Snow still covered most of the tarmac but was being lifted into large lorries.

Wareham Station had a sizeable crowd waiting on the up-platform. Experiences were being exchanged. Like the elements, the law had proved to be fickle, and no respecter of persons. Police had tried to deny passage to some but others had found themselves favoured. The train took no more than fifteen minutes to arrive and we progressed, humbled from Inter-City status to station-by-station crawl.

In the guard's van was a stretcher bearing the recumbent form of a sick man well wrapped in blankets and a fur hat askew on a lolling head. Beside him knelt his wife, her arched head advertising her concern as she leant over to comfort him, their half-grown son trotting aimlessly around the limited space. Against the grill separating luggage van from corridor leant the escorting nurse. Back towards me, sitting on a stack of baggage, was a figure identifiably medical.

He turned and I was able to recognise a physician of my acquaintance, bound to London for a meeting, and now providing help, if only in the assurance of his presence of a doctor. He turned over the pages of the case-notes which disclosed that the man was destined for the neurosurgical unit at Southampton, in coma with intracranial tumour.

I tried to mutter sympathy to the anxious wife and moved on. My being yet another doctor seemed an intrusion. I wondered how the patient would fare in a hospital crippled by a mindless strike of workers. Then back to London, still shod in gumboots, in time for a committee meeting – to the disbelief of colleagues – and surgery the following day.

Kimmeridge seascape, from Smedmore Hill to the Clavell Tower, with the English Channel forming the horizon.

Road-clearing operations were now making general progress across the county but on Thursday, 23 February it was necessary to fly fodder to a farm near Maiden Newton. These flights were co-ordinated by the Ministry of Agriculture and a naval helicopter pilot reported that food was badly needed in the remote village of Hooke which still remained completely isolated in the hills towards Beaminster. Telephone calls, to the post office and a school, established that they could last out another day, by which time it seemed the road would be opened. The snow was starting to thaw, though this brought its own troubles in the north of the county, with melt-waters from the River Stour threatening to flow through homes at Hammoon, where Wessex Water Authority issued sandbags.

By 17.00 hours on Friday, 24 February, all main roads in the county were declared to be open, but villagers in Hooke found they were still cut off. In desperation they prepared to walk to Beaminster. Elsewhere, the problems were being solved, and the police stood down the Control Centre at lunchtime. Over the weekend, the principal worry was at West Bay, where the sea wall had been washed away, and an evacuation plan was prepared but favourable tides enabled the breach to be sealed. It had been a week when the weather had been the only topic and events had been uncomfortably elemental.

1986

The Latter-day Siege
of Corfe Castle

Talk this Christmas was of our brave part in the post-Chernobyl tale of the invasion of the West Country by an army of hippies. Hysteria raged unchecked as reports reached London of a threat described by a Government minister, addressing Parliament, as a challenge to society from 'medieval brigands'. One of our national tabloid newspapers had no doubt that this could be the end of life as we knew it, with an assembly of 'travellers' on former Stoney Cross Airfield in the New Forest being described as 'the worst trouble spot in the world today'.

The cataclysmic hyperbole accompanied them westwards as the 200-strong band blazed a zigzag trail that took in four counties as they were escorted and outnumbered – on a two-to-one basis – by police minders. Above them the police helicopters reconnoitred and predicted where their colleagues might be heading. 'You'll all be living like this in ten years' time,' an itinerant pronounced from his roadside squat in a vehicle that was no longer utilising the invention of the wheel. 'Will the building societies really yield us up to our destiny?' I asked at the time.

Others from the lost generation opted for a gap-month to wear their tee-shirts proclaiming 'DHSS World Tour'. The media followed as sightings were reported from Guadeloupe, Mexico, and around the West Indies. The local story grew ever bigger in the telling as the secret unfolded of the heroic defence of the Isle of Purbeck against the hippie hordes. Road-blocking farmers were heard boasting in the Silent Women and the Halfway Inn that they had been armed. 'It was just like being back in the Home Guard,' said one of Dad's Army.

Farmers, the cynics noticed, fielded like against like. The oncoming influx of unroadworthy and untaxed vehicles were met with an assembly of unroadworthy and untaxed vehicles. Ditches were dug across de jure and de facto access points. Timber, brushwood, loads of silage and blocks of limestone were dragged or dumped behind chained gates. The Forestry Commission joined in the operation and placed their red fire tenders as road blocks to defend the front-line and Wareham.

Southwards, with their backs against the sea, the Army had the rearguard task of simply locking gates and posting sentries to protect the Lulworth Ranges and its vulnerable ranks of battle tanks. 'Tanks are their own justification,' an officer said, relishing the thought that the rebel force might liberate the Tank Museum.

That was the summer that was. The tourists seemed a bit miffed that Purbeck was closed and the siege of Corfe Castle was set to last a whole afternoon. That was the national perception but we knew better. In bars from the Sailor's Return in the west to the Bankes Arms in the east there were those who knew the truth. The War in the West truly lasted until Christmas and overgrown relics of the conflict could be found for the rest of the century. Some may soon be considered for scheduling as ancient monuments.

2000

Sir Laurence Whistler and the Christmas Kissing Bough

I was with Tony Poyntz-Wright in the churchyard at Curry Rivel, Somerset, just before Christmas in 2000. We were chatting to the vicar and had been discussing and comparing the windows of glass engraver Sir Laurence Whistler from Lyme Regis who had been knighted that year. It was no contest, I declared with pride: 'He's done a whole church down in Dorset at Moreton but he did have an empty canvas as it had been blown apart by the Luftwaffe.'

Sir Laurence Whistler whose windows adorn Moreton parish church.

The vicar said that he had been told that Whistler had died. I said he was still alive and that it must have been the knighthood that had caused Sir Laurence to be mentioned. In fact we were both right. He was dying that very day and I was stunned to see his intense eyes and handsome features, not unlike those of Kenneth Allsop, staring at me from the top of the obituary page in *The Times* a few days later.

I then realised that I had met him in Moreton without realising he was the visitor who arrived at the shell of a Georgian parish church and left it, a generation later, as a work of art without equal anywhere in the world. Before that claim to fame, back in Lyme for Christmas 1946, he had created a globe-shaped kissing bough for his Lyme home. 'It was the second

Christmas after the war,' he recalled, 'and neither box nor mistletoe could be found. Rosemary was slender and scanty.'

So he made his own bough with leaves and candles entwined around suspended apples:

> They glowed and came alive in the light of buoyant flames from fireplace and for me represented the symbol and crown of a Christmas in England. I was back home, from the Rifle Brigade, and the Christmas kissing bough represented the culture we had fought to protect.

It was a jingoistic festive statement, directly resulting from the Second World War, as the Christmas tree of Prince Albert of Saxe-Coburg was deliberately demoted in favour of the candlelit kissing bough of the English Middle Ages as the centrepiece for the living-room ceiling. Whistler worked from woodcuts by Joan Hassall and chose her globe as his model. An alternative, perhaps even earlier, used to be a crown.

Joan Hassall's woodcuts of the crown (top) and globe versions of the Christmas kissing bough revived by Laurence Whistler.

The latter is more practical for the low ceilings of cottages and ordinary homes. It is basically just half a globe, constructed as Sir Laurence described, but with nothing south of the equator, and its mistletoe suspended from the centre. Apples hang from the outer ring.

For his post-war globe, Whistler formed five circles of wire as the framework, which would last for years, in a structure two feet across. One spiral became the equator and the other four were meridians of longitude. They met at the poles and were tied in the middle. Evergreen vegetation was then attached according to taste – minimally in Whistler's case – with spaces for eight candles being left around the equator. Another was placed down in the south pole. Ideally, bright red apples would have been chosen for hanging in the centre at the core of the Earth, suspended by coloured ribbon from the north pole.

'We had to make do with green ones,' Sir Laurence said, recalling the paucity of Christmas fare in those austerity years of restricted imports, fuel shortages and the coldest winters since the 1890s. 'It made us improvise. A golden ball or an orange would have done instead. The surface is important as you want the flames of the candles to reflect around it.'

The globe requires a strong hook in the ceiling and more wire or red braid to attach it firmly. Finally a bunch of mistletoe is attached. No problem finding that now, or in nature in Curry Rivel where it grows from a false acacia tree in the churchyard, or in the limes beside Moreton House, but it tends to grow less abundantly close to the sea. Our friends in the north used to have to manage their kissing without it. So mistletoe on the kissing bough, traditionally, was subject to availability.

Beneath it the young would embrace and kiss. Carols would be sung. Family kisses would be exchanged at bedtime on Christmas Eve.

As for the Moreton windows, these include Moreton House in a blizzard as the image for winter. The five windows of the apse take up the story of Saint Nicholas, the patron saint of children and Christmas, and were made to Whistler's design by the London Sand-blasting Decorative Glassworks, under the direction of L.W. Legg in 1958. 'It is pleasant to have worked one's way around a church,' Whistler commented.

Moreton windows with engraved glass scenes that are exemplars of the craft, with seasonal touches ranging from a flowering magnolia to Moreton House in a blizzard.